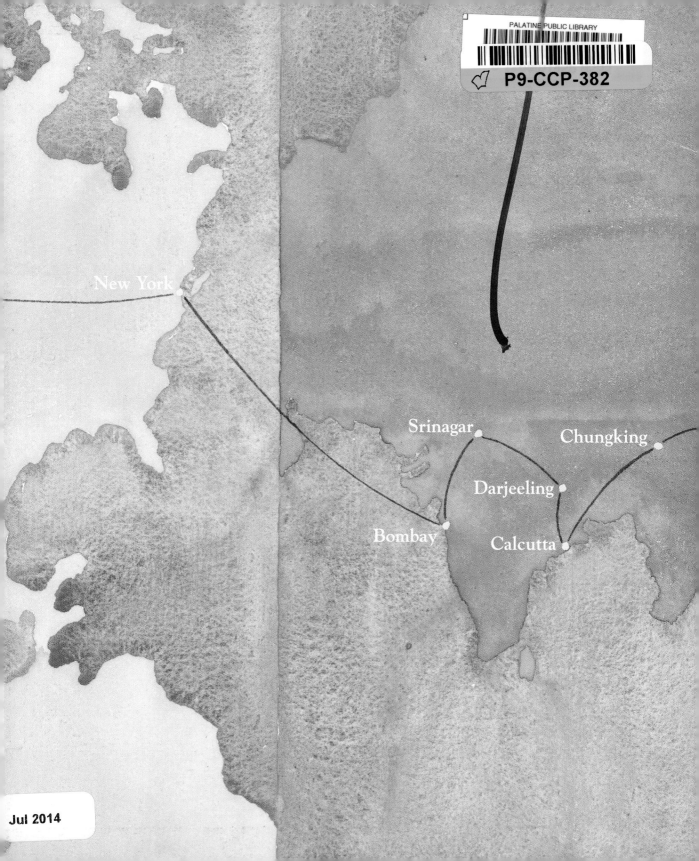

New York

Srinagar

Chungking

Darjeeling

Bombay

Calcutta

LEAVING
CHINA

LEAVING CHINA

An Artist Paints His World War II Childhood

James McMullan

ALGONQUIN   2014

Published by
Algonquin Young Readers
an imprint of Algonquin Books of Chapel Hill
Post Office Box 2225
Chapel Hill, North Carolina 27515-2225

a division of
Workman Publishing
225 Varick Street
New York, New York 10014

Cataloging-in-Publication Data is available from the Library of Congress.

10 9 8 7 6 5 4 3 2 1
First Edition

The names of the Indian and Chinese cities in the text are those that were used in the 1930s
through 1946, the period of this memoir. The current names are listed below.

Bombay—Mumbai
Calcutta—Kolkata
Cheefoo—Yantai
Chungking—Chonqing
Shantung Peninsula—Shandong
Yangchow—Yangzhou

For Kate,
You weren't there "then," but boy,
have you been there for me ever since.

LEAVING CHINA

CONTENTS

Throwing a Grape

MY EARLIEST MEMORY IS OF THROWING A GRAPE. I was a two-year-old playing on the stucco porch of a neighbor's house early one morning. I picked up a grape from a fruit bowl on the breakfast table and threw it for their German shepherd dog to chase. The grape bounced back off the wall and landed near me. The dog and I got to the grape at the same time, but I managed to close my chubby fingers around it just as the dog's jaws were about to claim the prize. The frustrated animal turned on me and bit me on the arm and on the back of the head. I remember in a dreamlike way the shouts and confusion of the adults when they called my parents and drove me to the hospital. It took fourteen stitches to close the gash on my head and six more for the wound on my arm. I don't remember the hospital or the pain, just the grape, the dog and the chaos. A little patch of hair never grew back on my head.

Looking back, I wonder if the dog attack had anything to do with the nervousness I exhibited during my childhood or whether I was simply destined to be a worried, anxious boy, German shepherd bites or not. I do know that my physical timidity in those early years was a concern to my father and mother and a great disappointment. This story of my peripatetic life during the Second World War, and of my family's beginnings in China, is also a story of that nervous boy gradually finding his strength in art and a way to be in the world that was not his father's or mother's idea of a man's life.

The Two Houses

M Y FATHER MANAGED A BRANCH OF THE FAMILY BUSINESS in Tsingtao for the first three years of my life. Then we moved to Cheefoo, another port on the Shantung peninsula, where the James McMullan Company had its main office.

I remember certain things about the big stone house in Cheefoo. The carpets were rectangles of warm gray bordered by the particularly Chinese pink. Complicated rattan chairs with wide arms had indentations for holding drinks. At the corner of the room by a window was a big black piano and near it a fancy-looking radio made of different kinds of wood and a green "eye" that would get brighter or dimmer as my father fiddled with the knobs. There were lots of cigarettes in silver boxes and flowers on the tables. Music played from the record machine and often my father would sing.

I remember my aunt Gladys's house next door. It was also a big stone house, but it smelled different from ours, like old milk, and there was randomness in the way that everything was placed as though it had been dropped in haste wherever it was. There was also a crucifix on the living-room wall. It was an object that was missing from our living room.

As I was later to understand, the two houses illustrated in their different styles—ours carefully put together for comfort and decorative effect, Gladys's ignored in order to concentrate on missionary tasks—the fact that the family history had created secular and religious branches.

The story of our family living a comfortable life in 1930s Cheefoo, China, had its beginnings in the bleak story of my grandparents, James and Lily McMullan, coming to China to work as missionaries.

James and Lily Arrive

MY GRANDPARENTS, JAMES AND LILY McMULLAN, met as missionaries in Yangchow, China, in 1887. He had come from Ballycastle in Ireland and she from Bristol in England. They had both joined the China Inland Mission, known as the C.I.M., an interdenominational Protestant Christian group proselytizing the faith in many parts of China. They were married and started their careers in Chungking, but because James developed respiratory problems in the humid climate of that interior city, he and Lily were sent by the mission to work in the port city of Cheefoo, in northern China, where the air was drier and cooler.

What James and Lily encountered when they arrived in 1888 was a land suffering from a series of devastating floods. Crops had been ruined and many people had been reduced to a meager diet of a little rice, wild plants from the countryside, fish, when they could get it, and seaweed from the beaches. It didn't help matters that many people were caught in the crossfire of disputes between two warlords, and there was rampant piracy along the coast, as well.

Despite the presence of other missionaries, James and Lily were left to their own devices to find a way to evangelize among the Chinese. They set up a mission house next to a busy road, hoping to interest people in their preaching and in the Mandarin bibles that they were prepared to distribute. They were still learning Mandarin, but they would stand by the road with an interpreter, asking people to come inside the house to hear the words of the gospels. The area residents were focused on survival and the entreaties had few takers.

The Cemetery Tower

A S THE MONTHS PASSED, it became apparent to James and Lily that their work must focus on helping the people in Cheefoo with their immediate problems before they could persuade them to accept the Christian message. They began spending most of their time walking with their interpreter out into the neighborhoods to hear what was happening in the actual lives of the villagers. Among the stories of disease and difficulties in finding food or work, one other horrendous story gradually emerged. Families were so destitute, struggling to feed all their children, that some parents, when a girl was born, took the infant and left her to die in a tower that was part of the cemetery on the outskirts of town. Because the Chinese valued sons above everything else as a means of future support, they did not abandon infant boys in this way. The McMullans had been aware on a theoretical level that infanticide was practiced in China and was a historical aspect of the culture, but to see it happening in such proximity was a cruelty they couldn't ignore.

My mother first told me this central story in the McMullan missionary history when I was about five. I was horrified at the idea of these murders but secretly relieved to be a boy, who would not have been chosen for this awful ending.

Saving the Babies

JAMES AND LILY ARRANGED FOR A WATCHMAN at the cemetery to alert them whenever a baby was taken to the tower. When a message came, they would hurry to the cemetery and take the baby back to their mission house to feed her and keep her alive. At first, some of the babies died from lack of mother's milk, but soon Lily realized she could engage poor women from the town to act as surrogate mothers and breast-feed the little girls.

I've often wondered if some of these surrogates turned out to be the actual mothers of these girls, secretly happy that their babies were alive and being cared for by foreigners who could afford to buy food.

James, with his background as a druggist's assistant in Ballycastle, had brought with him two books on basic medicine that he studied so that he could take care of many of the illnesses that occurred among the babies. Soon, villagers began to appear at the McMullans' door, asking James to heal them of their afflictions. This impromptu first-aid station was the beginning of a dispensary and, much later, a hospital that the family established. After a while, mothers who could not afford to feed their infant girls began to take them directly to James and Lily.

Many of the practical challenges, and the details of their lives as they took on the care of the babies, are lost in the mists of time. But one little fact may partly explain how they were able to afford the cost of these expanded responsibilities. A wealthy woman whom Lily had befriended back in Bristol and who believed in Lily's calling began to send the McMullans small checks. Small amounts of money went a long way in Cheefoo, China, and would have been a life-saving supplement to the modest allotment they got from the C.I.M. headquarters in Chungking.

This turn of events, bringing the babies back from the tower and caring for them, gave a sense of focus to James and Lily's lives and set them on a path that suited their talents. Yet this path eventually put them at odds with the China Inland Mission.

Building the Orphanage

WHEN THE NUMBER OF BABIES OUTGREW the small house that James and Lily lived in, they asked their friend in Bristol if she would donate the funds to build a modest orphanage. She sent the money, and the McMullans constructed a building that, along with dormitories for the girls, included a medical dispensary. They sited their structure next to the C.I.M. School, which had become an architectural hub for other missionary homes and church buildings. The school itself, which expanded over the years to include both a boys' and a girls' school, became one of the most famous English establishments in China. Among its graduates were the publisher Henry Luce, the playwright Thornton Wilder and the Olympic runner Eric Liddell, featured in the movie *Chariots of Fire*.

My father and my uncle and aunts went to the C.I.M. School. In my time, after a few months attending a kindergarten run by nuns at a French convent, I went to first grade, or "first form," as the English called it, at the school. Our house abutted the C.I.M. School playing fields, but I was taken to class by rickshaw the long way around because there was no practical way to climb over the high garden walls and walk across the fields.

Cutwork Embroidery

THE AREA AROUND CHEEFOO slowly recovered from the floods and the fields became fertile once more. This meant that families were no longer so destitute or forced to abandon their girl babies. The calls from the watchman at the cemetery to tell the McMullans to come to rescue an infant now stopped almost entirely.

Nevertheless, James and Lily realized that the group of girls under their care was growing older and they needed to plan for the girls' long-term futures. It was not enough to teach them English and to convert them to Christianity. The girls also needed a skill with which to earn money to survive and, perhaps, to help the orphanage itself survive. Because Cheefoo was in a part of China renowned for producing silk and cotton fabric, Lily and James decided to teach the young girls to make lace and to embroider in both silk and cotton. As the skills among the girls developed, one of the specialties of their output became table linens decorated with a style of embroidery called cutwork. This is an old technique of cutting shapes out of the cloth and binding and decorating the edges with embroidered designs.

As the years passed and the girls grew into their late teens, they were sought after as wives. They had learned English, knew a marketable skill and had been converted to Christianity, all attributes that were highly prized in the burgeoning economy of northern China. These girls, thrown away as persons of no value when they were infants, were now preferred over the young women who had been kept by their families.

Lily Finds Buyers

WHEREAS JAMES HAD A SPIRITUAL TEMPERAMENT that was well suited to his evangelical work, Lily had a practical and flexible turn of mind. She had organized the orphanage, purchased technical embroidery books and the simple machines they needed from England, and found teachers for the embroidery classes. Now she set about finding companies that might buy the tablecloths, napkins, handkerchiefs and gloves that the girls were producing. Traveling by ship from Cheefoo to Shanghai to meet with exporters, she persuaded one of them to start buying the embroidered products from the newly instituted James McMullan Company. The profits from this company were dedicated to supporting the orphanage and the dispensary.

Lily and James's decision to branch out into a business put them at odds with the China Inland Mission. The C.I.M. believed that its missionaries should concentrate on spreading the word of the Bible and that the McMullans were diluting the message with their commercial activities. James and Lily were convinced that the work they were doing with the orphanage and the embroidery school was crucial to the lives of the Chinese in the area, so they decided to leave the C.I.M. and found their own religious work organization, the Cheefoo Industrial Mission. It must have been a wrenching decision for them to leave the powerful organization that had brought them to China and that now questioned the core of their religious faith. Yet I think my grandmother, in particular, had the conviction to trust in her vision of Christian charity performed through practical acts. Lily McMullan was eventually credited with starting the whole embroidery industry in Shantung province.

The Four Siblings

DURING THE FIRST DECADE OF THE TWENTIETH CENTURY, James and Lily had four children. Gladys and Bobs, the older two, took after their mother in both looks and temperament: distinctive heavy-lidded eyes, almost Asian, strong round jaws, and in both cases, they saw the world in clear, practical terms. The younger siblings, Mary and James Jr., had the soulful blue eyes of their father and a tendency toward introspection and creativity. As they grew older Gladys became the helpmeet for her mother and assumed many of the duties of the school and orphanage; Bobs showed an early aptitude for entrepreneurship and by the time he reached thirty had created an entirely secular business, James McMullan Agencies, selling products for companies such as Ford Motor Cars, Metropolitan Life Insurance and Jardine Matheson Steamships. So, eventually, there was the embroidery exporting business, James McMullan Company, supporting the orphanage, dispensary and other religious work, and there was James McMullan Agencies supporting their employees and Bobs's, James's and Gladys's families. Mary married an oil-company executive in Shanghai and took up portrait painting.

James Jr. Brings Back a Bride

AFTER A BOYHOOD AS A STUDENT at the C.I.M. School and as a popular and darkly handsome young blade at the Cheefoo Club, James Jr., the youngest of the McMullan siblings, sailed to Vancouver, Canada, to study music at the university. Singing and playing the piano had always been his passion, and now he wanted to see whether he could make them his vocation. He spent about three years in Vancouver, studying and also working part time as a bond salesman. Sometime in his life, as either a student or a salesman, he met Rose Fenwick, a divorcée with two children. Rose had been raised on a ranch in Fort Steele, a town in the interior of British Columbia, and she had spent two years at Winchester College in England. She had lived there with Fenwick relatives who were members of the minor landed gentry, in a country manor called Abbot's Ann. This contrast between the rural simplicity of the Canadian ranch and the upper-class accoutrements of Winchester gave Rose's personality a kind of cowgirl-meets-duchess duality. She could be pragmatic and tough at times, and at other times imperious and critical. She was lovely to look at and capable of great charm and wit. I'm sure the latter attributes were much in evidence when she met the young man from China. The musician from Cheefoo and the divorcée from Fort Steele fell in love and, after a brief courtship, were married.

James, now a husband and the stepfather of a nine-year-old daughter and an eight-year-old son, decided that his musical career could wait. He would take his new family to China and assume a role in the family business.

Life in Cheefoo

BY THE TIME I WAS BORN, in 1934, the McMullan Company had been in existence for thirty-one years. The embroidery and lace the young women at the Industrial Mission were producing was being sold in America and England, and the demand was great enough that many of the workers were no longer orphans but simply young women and men who had been hired in the usual way. As the number of orphans waned and the needs of the orphanage were reduced, the proceeds from the James McMullan Company were increasingly used to support a new hospital and the church. The McMullan Agencies had also expanded, and their success was part of a generally booming economy in that part of China during the prewar years, providing a comfortable life for the family. We had house servants, gardeners, a rickshaw man and a chauffeur who drove our always new-model Ford or Dodge. My father was able to indulge his pleasure in buying the latest gramophone records, and my mother either had clothes sent from stores in America or had them made by a seamstress. The McMullans, when they weren't working, were part of the lively British, American and European social scene in Cheefoo that revolved around evening parties, lunches at the Cheefoo Club and, for our family, a cottage that we had built on a high bluff overlooking the ocean a few miles from the center of the city.

I remember our launch, which took us from the wharf in Cheefoo to the beach below our house on the bluff. It had a deep draft and had to anchor thirty or forty feet offshore, so strong Chinese men in the area were hired to carry the ladies and the children from the boat to the shore, as well as all the food that would make up our "tiffin," the colonial name for early lunch. The men in the family simply waded through the surf. We could see two huge rocks from the verandah of the cottage, one round and smooth that my father named "Mama Rock" and one tall and jagged that, of course, was "Papa Rock." These trips to the Bluff Cottage were my first experience of untamed nature.

My Mother in the Garden

I CAN REMEMBER FOLLOWING MY MOTHER, Rose, as she walked through the garden choosing the flowers she wanted the gardener to cut for the day's bouquets. The gardens surrounded the large, granite-block house. It had a spacious greenhouse where we would often sit in the morning to have tea and to eat a kind of pastry that was the closest approximation to a crumpet that our cook could devise. The house had big porches with bamboo blinds that could be rolled down for shade, and the kind of rattan furniture that has big swoopy arms. My father had acquired a St. Bernard dog whose size seemed overwhelming to me and, because of the dog attack earlier in my life, a little scary. But I was happy enough playing with our other dog, a Pekingese, which we had named Dee Gwa, or "sweet potato" in Mandarin. Something about the slow, deliberate pace at which my mother walked around the flowerbeds, choosing a blossom here, a blossom there, sticks in my mind in a way that other parts of the day do not. Perhaps those were the moments when her role as the mistress of the house was clearest and she was most comfortable. She oversaw the menus for our meals, but our cook was a strong-willed fellow who often seemed to get his way about what we ate.

My Father at the Piano

MY FATHER WAS STILL DEVOTED TO MUSIC, the piano and singing. In the late afternoons, home from the office, he sat at the keyboard and played and sang the hit songs of the day that he had heard over the radio or on records. The songs he loved he played over and over again, tinkering with the tunes and the tempo: "The Way You Look Tonight" and "When the deep purple falls over sleepy garden walls," as well as the songs from *Anything Goes*. He had a good singing voice and a fluid way of playing. Like so many musically inclined people of that time, he was enamored of the light, flowing style of the movie musicals. Those popular songs and movies influenced much of what my father and mother wore, what they drank, and how they arranged their social life. It was for them a special connection (and a style tutorial) to that fabulous world very far away from Cheefoo.

My father was a very English man in his manners and sense of propriety, but almost American in his feeling for clothes and glamour. He was able to take a magazine photo of a posh event in New York and a bolt of English cloth to his Chinese tailor, who made him an excellent copy of the dinner jackets he saw in the photo. This attraction to material things and to the lighthearted games of society, for which he was suited by temperament and talent, gave him pangs of guilt, since the saintly life of his parents was never very far from his mind, and the example of his missionary sister, Gladys, was only a house away. Occasionally I would overhear my father proclaiming that they must stop all this partygoing and lead more Christian lives.

These memories of late afternoon, when I played with my toys as my father sat at the baby grand and casually sang or experimented, doodling out some variation on the melody, happened at that moment when the sun coming through the tall windows would be carved into clear rectangles on the carpet into which I could steer my trucks and cars as if they were entering a city of light.

The Musical

THE CENTER FOR SOCIAL LIFE in the town was the Cheefoo Club, a sprawling series of buildings and patios and tennis courts set on the beach. My father was popular at the club, not only because he was the Irishman with the soulful eyes who played a graceful game of tennis, but also because he wrote and directed musical revues that were performed on the club's stage. The stories he wrote were filled with inside jokes about Cheefoo life and personalities, and he stole unashamedly in much of his music from the tunes of popular songs. He cast the productions with friends and family members, whether or not they could sing or dance or act, even giving my half sister, Bette, who was chubby and self-conscious, a part. Nevertheless, despite the hokey lyrics and story and the not-so-original melodies, the productions were taken very seriously, and as writer, composer, director and one member of the two-piece band, my father ran a tight ship. After months of costume sewing and rehearsals, the show opened as the big event of the season and was always counted as a great success, since the half of the community in the production was related to the half that was in the audience.

The American Navy Visits

B Y THE EARLY THIRTIES Cheefoo had become a regular port for the American navy to visit in the summer, and their arrival signaled the start of the social season. Their cruisers and destroyers, lying in clear sight in the harbor, were a visual reminder of the "Good Will" sea power of the United States. Of course, Cheefoo was also a very pleasant summer resort city where officers and sailors could get off their ships to relax. The Bund (named, like the avenue in Shanghai, by German traders earlier in the century), the wide street that ran along the shore, was crowded with small curio shops and bars that catered to the pleasures and distractions of the ordinary seamen, while the porches of the Cheefoo Club were often awash in the crisp white uniforms of ensigns, lieutenants and commodores. The bands from the ships often performed concerts at the club, and boxing and wrestling matches were arranged between navy men and the more athletic civilians in the community.

The Drowned Man

I SPENT MUCH OF MY TIME with my Chinese amah, who spoke rudimentary English, but who often said things to me in Mandarin. Because of this mélange of words, I had difficulty keeping the two languages I was hearing in separate categories. My speech was basically in English, sprinkled here and there with Chinese expressions.

My father, with his musical ear, intensely absorbed by languages and fluent in Chinese and Japanese, encouraged me to speak Chinese. The little I knew as a six-year-old would be gone by the time I was twelve.

I spent many afternoons with my amah walking to the beach near the house. I remember one of these walks, particularly, because a crowd had gathered along the water's edge to look at something. I sensed that whatever they were looking at was something I didn't want to see, and I resisted Amah when she tugged at me to get a closer look. She was stronger than I and soon we were jostling through the crowd to get to the center. There, splayed out on the sand, was the body of a Chinese man, grotesquely frozen into the contorted position of his last struggle with the ocean. He was a gray specter, almost like a piece of driftwood, dramatically inanimate in a way I have never forgotten.

There was so much anxiety pushed under the rug in those years, so much hushed talk of atrocities committed by the Japanese or by the warlords. I only caught bits and pieces of these stories, but it was enough to give me a sense of dying and death that was out there somewhere beyond the safe enclave of our family. Now I had seen my first dead human and it brought into sharper focus the fuzzy dread of the stories overheard.

The Japanese Army Arrives

Because our family printed the local paper and was connected to Reuters and other news services, there was a lot of war talk in our house. My father and mother tried to keep the worst news out of the dinner conversation, but I heard enough to know that Germans were doing bad things in Europe and that the Japanese army was in our part of China. On some days we could hear the distant thud of artillery. As that army got closer to Cheefoo, my parents had no choice but to tell me that the Chinese would have to surrender and that the Japanese would take over the town. They assured me that, because we were British and not at war with Japan, we would be safe. I was only four years old, but my parents' explanation about our neutrality didn't seem to me like a strong defense against people who could make the Chinese surrender without a fight.

The day finally came when the army rumbled into town. We stayed in our house, but the sound of the tanks rattling along and grinding up the pavement of the main street was easy enough to hear. The marching troops would occasionally let out a coordinated shout that even to a young child was clearly the yowl of the conqueror.

The Japanese Commandant

BY 1937, MY FATHER AND MY UNCLE BOBS were among the leaders of the British and American community in Cheefoo. As such, they were ordered to appear before the Japanese commandant to hear the rules and restrictions that he was imposing on the movement and behavior of the neutral inhabitants of the town. Britain and the United States, although in a contentious relationship with Japan, had not yet declared war against it. The commandant instituted small tariffs on the export or import of goods, and British, Americans and Europeans were required to bow to any Japanese soldier or officer they encountered. Because the tariffs made letting businesses continue to operate more profitable than shutting them down, Japanese interference, at first, was minimal. As long as some ships were sailing to and from the U.S. and England, the McMullan Company was able to sell its embroidery and to import cars.

Because I was always protected from any direct information about the Japanese control of our lives, I became ever more sensitive to the tone of my parents' conversations. My parents' mood when my father returned from the meeting with the commandant was both relieved and resigned. The company could continue operating, but, despite our neutral status, it was clear that we were virtual prisoners of the Japanese.

The Road Blockades

ONE CHANGE THAT AFFECTED THE DAILY LIFE of the British and Americans was obvious enough that I couldn't be shielded from it. This was the institution of roadblocks that the Japanese military set up to check individuals' papers, particularly the medical document that proved you had been inoculated against cholera. Because I was inevitably going to experience these roadblocks on one of my rickshaw trips along the streets on my way to school, my mother explained to me what they were. The roadblocks would be moved around to various locations, usually somewhere along the heavily traveled street that ran by the beach. If you were stopped at one and didn't have the appropriate forms, you would stand in line to be injected with the same needle that had been used on those who had gone before you. This ritual of the barricades was also part of the effort by the Japanese to humiliate foreigners. The soldiers would bark out orders in Japanese, getting angrier and angrier that we didn't understand. The chance that any of us might have forgotten our papers or that a particular soldier might decide not to accept them added greatly to the anxiety of traveling in the city.

When I was taken to school or to a friend's house, I remember sitting scrunched back under the canopy of the rickshaw, hoping that we would not come upon surly soldiers standing by their trestles and barbed wire. My rickshaw man and I were stopped only once, and the Japanese sergeant accepted the papers that we produced. Aunt Gladys, however, was caught in this Cholera Inoculation dragnet and subjected to injection by public needle. She was fortunate to endure only a swollen arm and a feverish day.

The Night Runners

URING THIS TIME, my teenaged half-siblings, Bob and Bette, were sent away to study in Canada, missing much of the tension of living under the military occupation. But life for the rest of the family continued as a kind of shadow-play version of what it had been before the Japanese took over the town. Superficially, we went through the same round of work, school and recreation, but it was now darkened by the presence of the army everywhere. There were the soldiers at the barricades, of course, and at the doors of all the buildings the army hierarchy had commandeered. Other soldiers drove along the streets in their dun-colored staff cars; occasionally they rumbled along in their half-tank vehicles. They were also present on the shore. I remember several picnics on the beach when squads of soldiers dressed only in sumo-style loincloths ran by, grinning at us challengingly as they passed. My strongest memory, though, is of the night runners. Detachments of Japanese infantry, led by a soldier carrying a flaming torch, would pound down the narrow street just beyond our garden wall in a seemingly endless drumbeat of stomping boots and guttural chants.

I lay in bed listening to this ominous percussion and imagining many of the bad things my parents had assured me were never going to happen.

The Chinese Scrolls

BECAUSE OF THE ROADBLOCKS, my parents stopped sending me out so often with the rickshaw man to visit friends or to attend birthday parties. I still went to the C.I.M. School, which was very close, but many days I stayed inside the house with my mother or my amah, reading *Winnie the Pooh* or the Oz books, visiting the servants in the kitchen or idly looking at the complicated scenes depicted in the painted scrolls on the living-room walls. These were delicate watercolor depictions of craggy mountains piercing swirling clouds. Near the bottom of the scrolls, tiny clusters of figures sat in pavilions, contemplating life, or drinking tea by rivers and bamboo groves. They were painted in subtle variations of brown and ochre but seemed amazingly full of air and space. I was fascinated by the way brushstrokes could become rocky outcroppings or twisted tree trunks or flowers or flowing robes. The images were all so quiet and subdued but somehow so alive.

Later, when I was about twelve and had some art materials, I would experiment with a brush and ink, trying to make marks that looked something like the bamboo I had studied in the scrolls. I taught myself how to put pressure on the brush to suggest the thickened joint of the bamboo stalk and to flick the brush in the right way to create the bladelike shape of the leaves. Making marks that looked like people was still too hard.

The Costume Ball

NEWS FROM THE WAR IN EUROPE grew worse and the government in Tokyo became more belligerent; yet my father went to work to book someone on a Lloyd Triestino ship or make the occasional Ford car or truck sale or sell a Manufacturers Life insurance policy.

In the evenings my mother and father still attended dinner parties, dances, bridge parties and the ever more frequent and extravagant costume balls. As I look at photographs of these elaborate masquerades, put together as the inevitable war grew closer and closer, I wonder if my parents and their friends hoped that by dressing up as a pirate, a hobo, a clown or a gypsy they might successfully fool impending misfortune. It was still the good colonial life but lived with a desperate edge.

At the Dock

THE BAD NEWS CONTINUED and a more widespread war seemed inevitable. By the spring of 1940 there was no longer any attempt by the military authorities to disguise the fact that we were under their total control. In the summer of 1941 the British Consulate in Cheefoo warned all British nationals to leave the country.

The warning came almost too late. When my father went to the Japanese headquarters to get visas to travel to Shanghai, where he had booked passage to America for my mother and me, he was told that his wife and son could leave, but he, being of military age, could not. He managed to convince the authorities that he simply would be accompanying us to Shanghai and would return to Cheefoo. We packed up our clothes and a few household belongings, but most of our belongings we left behind in order to support the charade that my father would return.

My father, mother and I left on a small ship for the voyage to Shanghai, but not before a soldier, examining our luggage, threw out my father's precious stamp collection. He had started it when he was in his teens, and it contained rare stamps from the first mail service in China, as well as stamps that his father had saved on envelopes from all over the world in the 1880s.

My Uncle Bobs remained in Cheefoo to look after the family interests, but there was really not much he could save. Less than a year later, he was arrested, and he died in a Japanese prison.

USS President Coolidge

WHEN WE ARRIVED, Shanghai was under siege by the Japanese army, although the Chinese and international forces still had a tenuous hold on the city. When the cab took my parents and me along the Bund to our hotel, the people we saw from the car window looked frantically animated. Their running and pushing behavior gave the street an unreal atmosphere of tension mixed with a determination to ignore the reality of the situation. Our hotel room was first class and the service was impeccable. In the restaurant where we went for dinner, an ethereal-looking woman in a long, silver gown played a harp on a dais at the end of the room. The menu gave no sense that the blockade had limited the offerings: I ordered one of my special treats, fresh asparagus, and my parents had caviar.

Under the surface of calm there was a desperate crush to find passage out of China. Because of our contacts through the Cheefoo company, we had been fortunate enough to secure a cabin on the USS *President Coolidge*, one of the big, modern ships of the American President Lines and the second-to-last ship to carry passengers out of Shanghai before the Japanese army overran the city.

Two days after arriving in Shanghai we took the launch out to the ship. Then my father, after seeing our stateroom and saying a long, emotional good-bye to my mother and me, walked back down the gangplank. I was distracted from the significance of the good-byes by the novelty and excitement of being on a real ocean liner and watching from the side of the ship as a tugboat began pulling us out of the harbor. When I turned away from the tug I saw my mother's eyes following the receding figure of my father standing in the back of the launch. I had never seen such sadness and apprehension on her face.

My Father Joins the British Army

MY FATHER BEGAN WRITING to my mother almost as soon as the *Coolidge* had left the dock. My mother would read parts of his letters to me, leaving out what I guessed were the mushy parts. Later he would write to me directly.

As he explained in his first letter, he reported to the British Army recruiter in Shanghai the day after we sailed. After taking a physical exam and a test of his fluency in Mandarin, he was accepted and, after training, would be granted a commission as second lieutenant. The Mandarin test was significant because it probably meant that he would be trained to work with the Chinese Free Army operating behind the Japanese lines.

In this early period of his letters, before the military censors restricted what he could say about his movements, he was able to tell us that he had traveled to Rangoon and then to a training camp somewhere in Burma.

> There are a lot of friendly officers here who took me in hand when I first arrived and showed me the ropes although I still have a lot to learn. My civilian muscles are slowly adapting to the training. One doesn't worry about the almost constant rain here and we have been going out for P.T. and walks and runs and barricade climbing regardless of the weather. Actually P.T. is not compulsory for Officers, but Junior Officers like myself are supposed to turn out each morning with the men—as an example.
>
> Today I came back from a fourteen mile "jaunt" with my clothes all caked with mud after sitting in a ditch half full of slime. My poor Bearer, "Sunday," (a phonetic approximation of his Madrassee name) is sitting outside my room now scraping mud off my boots and puttees and frowning at the idea of the tremendous polishing job he has on his hands.

The last piece of specific military information he could include in his letters was that he was being assigned to a place close to where he had started, thus hinting at the area around Shanghai.

White Houses and Green Lawns

OUR VOYAGE TO THE UNITED STATES was a wonderland of American, up-to-date details—deco chrome railings on the grand staircase going down to the main dining room, sleek blond wood on the walls of our stateroom, murals of Hawaiian scenes in which hula girls, surfboard riders and palm trees had been evoked with swooping unnaturalistic geometric shapes. Grapefruit (which I had never eaten before) was served on blue glass dishes that looked like rings in a pond. The behavior of the waiters and crewmen also signaled that we had entered a different world. They talked to us and smiled in a straightforward manner, not with the averted gazes and deferential tone that I had known as the demeanor of servants in China. My mother and I were amazed by the view of San Francisco as the *President Coolidge* sailed under the Golden Gate Bridge. The city looked clean and white and modern to me, very different from the dusty, worn streets and buildings I was used to in Cheefoo. Steaming into San Francisco Bay, I felt as though I had arrived at a shimmering city of Oz.

We stayed a night in San Francisco before taking the train to Seattle to meet my father's sister, my aunt Mary. She had left China six months before and was already ensconced in a white stucco bungalow set into the rectangle of a mani-cured green lawn in a neighborhood filled with equally rectilinear structures. When I walked on the smooth cement sidewalks of her neighborhood in Seattle and saw the shiny cars lined up in the driveways, it was hard to believe that there was a war being fought anywhere in the world. Or that back in Cheefoo, Japa-nese soldiers were taking my uncle off to a rat-infested prison cell. The inside of the house was not so well tended, since Mary was making a haphazard adjust-ment to life without servants. She asked my mother and me to stay on with her; but after two weeks of trying unsuccessfully to help Mary bring some order into the daily dishevelment of the house, my mother decided it was time for us to move on to her parents' home.

Bad Nights in Grand Forks

MY MOTHER AND I TOOK A TRAIN to Vancouver, British Columbia, and another to Grand Forks, in the interior of the province. Her parents' house was very different from Aunt Mary's in Seattle. It was an ordinary farmhouse, a little worse for wear and surrounded by a scraggly lawn and a broken sidewalk in the middle of the beaten-up town. The interior of the house had an airless fustiness, and the bathroom was permeated with the smell of iodine from the large sea sponges that sat on the bathtub tray. Curling linoleum lay on the floor. My grandfather, Arthur, was a taciturn man who had been a rancher and local magistrate before he retired. His wife, Nan, was a calm, quiet woman with a bemused edge to her manner, perhaps the result of being a French-Canadian in an Anglo world.

My mother and I moved in, grateful to have a haven in which to regroup. The meaning of the flight from Cheefoo and my separation from my father, now that the novelty of the trip had worn off, began to sink in. My mother and I were now wanderers, not yet attached to any particular place and without any clear destination. Seattle and the security of calm America had seemed reassuring for a moment, but we had moved on. Perhaps Grand Forks with my grandparents would be a home for us, perhaps not. At this time my brother Bob had enlisted in the Canadian Air Force and was training in England. We had seen my sister briefly when we passed through Vancouver. She had a job at a military parts depot and turned down my mother's invitation to join us.

For the first few nights, when I lay in bed I became convinced that if I fell asleep, I would never wake up. On these bad nights I climbed out of bed and went down to the living room, where I found my grandfather, sitting in his overstuffed chair, listening to the radio. Grandad Arthur was puzzled by my fears, but he comforted me as best he could. After drinking a cup of cocoa, I climbed back up the stairs to the bedroom too exhausted to resist sleep.

The Wrong Accent

M Y MOTHER TOOK ME TO the local public school in Grand Forks and enrolled me in second grade. When the teacher asked me to stand and read a passage from a textbook, the class giggled at my precise enunciation and the long vowels of my English accent. The teacher, a young girl from the countryside, interrupted me to ask, "Where, exactly, are you from?" I replied, "China." The students howled, thinking this was even more of a joke. The teacher, getting into the spirit of the crowd, told me to sit back down and that I had better learn to speak English "properly."

This public rebuke by the teacher gave the natural bullies in the class permission to push me around at recess and to grab the paper bag containing my lunch. Many of the students were the sons and daughters of a displaced Russian religious sect, the Doukhobors, who were particularly large, rough and physical. Of course, my precise manner of speaking and fancy-sounding accent made me the "Little Lord Fauntleroy" they were happy to bring down a few pegs. I went home day after day, tearful, shaken and hungry, to report these daily skirmishes to my mother. Wishing that I were made of sterner stuff, she encouraged me to "buck up" and to "ignore the rascals." After two weeks, however, she realized that this particularly provincial teacher and this particularly loutish group of kids were presenting me a challenge I was never going to overcome by "bucking up." She took me out of the school and engaged a tutor to teach me at home. She also enrolled me in boxing lessons at the local YMCA. I wish I could report that I found my inner hero in these once-a-week bouts of sparring, but I was consistent to the end, remaining the sissy kid who selflessly gave everyone else in the class the taste of victory.

Before long, I was saved from enduring this agony by my mother's decision that she had had enough of this backwater town and its lack of a smart set. She packed us up, and soon we were on our way to visit her sister on an island off the west coast of Canada.

The Beautiful House

SALT SPRING ISLAND LIES IN THE STRAIT OF GEORGIA, between the Canadian mainland and three-hundred-mile-long Vancouver Island. It is the largest of the Gulf Islands in the strait and is reached by boat from the city of Vancouver. For some time it had been a popular resort and second-home community, particularly for people from the inland provinces who had made money and wanted to live near water. Ella, my mother's sister, and her husband, Bish Wilson, had sold the coal mines they owned in Fernie, British Columbia, and had just completed a house on a shelf of land bordering the sea that represented the trophy and pleasure of their new, early retirement.

After driving past acres of property, we reached the house by a road that curved down a steep hill. The large structure was an odd but satisfying combination of stucco, stone and cedar siding. Metal mullioned windows had been set into dormers in its complicated roof. The bathrooms had sinks set atop chrome legs and faucets with a geometric simplicity that seemed the essence of modernity. All the enameled appliances were a subtle shade of blue, as were the tile floors. It was the most beautiful house I had ever seen.

As I walked across the generous spaces, ran my hands along the rough texture of the plastered walls, smelled the cedar paneling in the bedroom, saw the light streaming in through the modern stained glass of the tall entryway, I felt that all the attention to detail and to some central idea guiding the choices made the house seem strong and rooted to its piece of earth. I realized, even then, how much comfort I found in the intelligence of my visual surroundings.

Ella cooked a grand meal to welcome my mother and me: roast beef and Yorkshire pudding, tomatoes and spinach from the garden and a rich dessert called "floating islands." The adults drank many whiskies and I had a glass of milk with my dinner. I had never tasted milk so creamy.

My Cousin Alan

THE NEXT DAY MY SLIGHTLY YOUNGER COUSIN, Alan, walked me down to the bay to take me out in the dugout canoe that he'd found washed up on the beach. It was only half carved out and, because there was a warp in the log, very tippy. It was easy to understand why the Indians in the nearby community abandoned it. It was fun to try to keep it from rolling over.

Alan jumped from rock to rock, leading me around his domain of reefs and bays. I followed timidly, more interested in the small fish and crabs I saw caught in the tidal pools than in the leaping contest. Alan urged me to risk what I was clearly uncomfortable doing, but he did it in a way that didn't seem unkind. He was a boy with a harelip and a small body who had undergone his own trials, so he was patient with me.

Despite the differences between Alan's physicality and my timid, introspective personality, we found a way in the next few weeks to get along and to have fun with each other. Alan even managed to help me gain some athletic confidence and to lose the frozen demeanor I had arrived with. No doubt, he was motivated to be friendly with me in part because I was the only playmate within two miles, but whatever the reasons, we became buddies and assumed our roles. He was the short, scrappy daredevil teaching me how to shoot cans with a .22 rifle and how to row the dinghy fast enough to troll for salmon, while I was the skinny reader, introducing him to Bulldog Drummond detective stories and telling tales of life in China.

The Moment on the Reef

DESPITE THE COMFORT OF MY FRIENDSHIP WITH ALAN, I needed time to be alone. In one of the reefs near the house, caves had been formed in the rock by the bubbles of gas within the volcanic lava that had originally created the formation. One of my favorite solitary pastimes was to explore all these different-size apertures and find one to huddle in and to simply stare out at the ocean. It challenged my nerves and agility a little, since getting from one cave to the next involved navigating stretches of steep, smooth rock, but somehow the thrill of the caves was sufficient to motivate me. As I crouched in a cave, looking out at the dark water, I sometimes thought about my father and what he had described about living in the jungle in his latest letter. More often though, I simply tried to imagine all the things that must be happening under the waves. One day I was surprised by something I'd never imagined. The surface of the water lapping not eight feet away from me was broken by a huge killer whale, rising smoothly from below, first the dorsal fin and then the whole thirty- or forty-foot length of its body. It gently rocked against the reef as though scratching an itch or, more probably, scraping away the barnacles that had attached themselves to its flanks. I sat utterly motionless, partly from fear but mostly because I didn't want this extraordinary moment to pass. I felt that if my arms had been just a little bit longer I could have reached out and touched the fin. After a few minutes the black massiveness of the whale sank out of sight as seamlessly as it had appeared and I ran back to the house to tell everyone what I had seen.

After a month, my mother decided to go to Vancouver to look for work, but since I was obviously happy here with the Wilsons and they were willing to keep me, she left me in Salt Spring to start the fall term at the local public school with Alan.

The Russian Artist

I HAD NEVER EXHIBITED ANY OF MY FATHER'S MUSICALITY, but it turned out that I had a good ear for spoken accents. I also had an accommodating personality and was able quickly to adjust my speaking voice so that it mirrored the voices I heard around me. After only a few months with the Wilsons I had lost most of my crisp English speech and had taken on more of the flat vowels of the Canadian dialect. This new semi-Canadianness in the way I sounded made it much easier this time around for me to fit in with the other students in the school. I also discovered that telling my schoolmates stories of my past in China, embellished with details about warlords and pirates, kept a certain amount of bullying at bay.

The trips home after school were another adventure. The school bus took Alan, two neighbor children and me to a bus stop three miles from the Wilsons' house and, unless it was raining or very cold and Ella used precious rationed gas to pick us up in her car, we walked the rest of the way home. The four of us dawdled and teased and joked our way up the hills and along the farm fields, counting deer and always looking out for the dangerous cougar that never appeared. The only house we passed was a small modern bungalow set in a valley next to the steep road we climbed. We had heard that the man who owned it was a Russian aristocrat and an artist. We always hoped to see him outside his house exhibiting some weird behavior worthy of someone who had fled from Russia, possibly under dark circumstances. And then, one sunny afternoon, there he was, standing at an easel on his patio, painting a landscape. The others were disappointed that he seemed so normal and matter of fact in the way he calmly put one stroke after another on the canvas; I was fascinated with my first view of an artist at work. My companions quickly decided to move on, but I hung back for a little while to watch this simple process that seemed strangely magical.

Quartered in a Buddhist Temple

IN MY FATHER'S LETTERS TO ME, along with his frequent expressions of hope that I was becoming "a strong little fellow" who was improving his math skills and his athletic performance, he included colorful details of his life in remote parts of the Chinese countryside.

> The building, which I am converting to a field Operation Center, is an old temple and one section is crammed full of Golden Idols. There is a big fellow with three eyes at the door but I feel he makes a poor impression on new-comers, so I have put him at the back and replaced him with a somewhat smug effigy which holds out its hand in a cautionary attitude as if to say "have you had your oatmeal today?" The village elder, who often visits me and brings me wonderful Chinese dishes, told me to remove the idols if I wished but I hesitate to perpetrate such an iconoclasm, especially at Chinese New Year's time. In any case I have developed considerable affection for a large, fierce Warrior-God which sits in one corner brandishing a sword.
>
> As a British officer I am accorded great respect. When I walk through the village the splendor of my brass-buttoned uniform creates such a sensation that I am followed from place to place by a group of children.

Leaving Salt Spring

O N ONE OF MY MOTHER'S VISITS TO SALT SPRING, she asked me how I was doing with my Latin, a subject the Salt Spring school curriculum, unlike English schools, didn't start till fourth grade. (I was eight, and still in third grade.) Hearing this news, her duchess side was aroused, and she launched into a general criticism of Canadian public schools, my fading colonial accent, and my new attempts at cheekiness. In short, my mother was convinced that I was losing my connection to my English father and had become a Canadian boor. This was far from the truth, since I was still essentially the nervous child she had brought from Cheefoo, with a new veneer of up-to-the-minute slang and a conspiratorial repartee with my cousin.

Perhaps prompted by a competitive relationship with her sister, Ella ("Public school may be good enough for Alan, but my son needs an English-style education"), and much heavy drinking over the visit, my mother convinced herself that the Salt Spring school was not educating me properly and that she must take me back to Vancouver and enroll me in a boarding school.

The decision stunned me like a bad bolt out of the blue, because my nine months with the Wilsons had begun to feel like normalcy and stability, a first since we'd left Cheefoo. My mother's erratic decisions in Grand Forks had given me a taste of how she operated without my father's guidance, but this new, sudden upheaval in my life was particularly confusing and sad for me. I hated leaving Salt Spring.

The Wilsons drove us to the dock in Ganges, the main village on the island, and we boarded the boat for Vancouver.

The Vaulting Horse

M Y MOTHER ENROLLED ME AS A BOARDER at St. George's School in Vancouver, which did its best to emulate the British model of public school education and character building. The school itself was a slightly worn-down Tudor-style building with the appropriately musty hallways and a chapel that smelled of furniture polish and slowly molding hymnals. I found myself behind the other students in Latin but caught up quickly in French, as something about the sounds of the language intrigued me. I was also able to write a coherent paragraph, albeit too filled with flowery adjectives and show-off words.

The school philosophy put great emphasis on sports as a way to mold exemplary young men, and every afternoon was devoted to some sort of physical activity. I survived the soccer games by using my running speed to fake my way out of most of the ball action, but gymnastics was another story. I was simply too fearful and out of touch with my body to send it into the arcs or flips or hanging movements demanded of me. Among the physically inept boys I was one of the two worst. Over and over again I stumbled and balked at the vaulting horse, only to be sent to the back of the line to make another futile try. The vaulting horse became the center of my nightmares of gymnastic torture. I begged my mother to somehow get me excused from gym. She was contemptuous of my entreaties but she finally wrote a letter to the school that succeeded in getting me released.

Gone were the terrors of gym, but I paid a heavy price in my sense of having failed to live up to my father's hopes for me. Yet, another more devious and pragmatic part of me recognized that I could control my life to some degree, even if it took begging my mother to write a letter. And I had an increasing awareness that maybe these sporting values so prized at grammar school would not be the transcendent values of my future life. I hoped, and began to believe, that there was a world out there in which one's success in life did not depend on one's vaulting skills.

Weekends with Rose

On most weekends, I stayed with my mother at her modest apartment. She had gone through the money she brought from China, and my father's allotment from his officer pay only sporadically made it past the red tape in China. Her small salary as a bookkeeper at a military parts depot was now most of her income. It puzzled me that we went from our easy life in China to "scraping by" in Canada, but I later learned that all of our assets had been frozen in Cheefoo banks. My mother assuaged her depression about her new penury and about being separated from her husband by drinking. It was a problem that had started in China and that my father referred to in his letters somewhat obliquely as hoping "she is being a good girl."

When I was holed up in the apartment for the weekends with my mother, I saw her slip into the kitchen surreptitiously to refill her glass with gin. Her speech would start to slur and her fake English accent increased until she became the Bitchy Duchess. During this period I finally admitted to myself that her drinking was real and frequent, and not just a party thing that I used to hope would never happen again. I felt that when my mother drank she went somewhere far away from me.

These weekends were not entirely grim. We sometimes visited the zoo or went to the movies together and saw pictures like *This Is the Army, Mr. Jones!*, and I was smitten with the glamour of these big wartime productions. Yet I sensed that my mother's life was really lived during the week and that I was some kind of interruption to it. There were phone calls at the apartment, conversations in which she responded with evasions and euphemisms or with laughter and a teasing flirtiness. She was only forty-one and still a very attractive woman, but it was hard for me to accept the idea that my mother was involved with men other than my absent father. Yet somehow I knew that whoever was on the other end of those calls was not a woman.

My Father Is Reassigned

THIS LETTER FROM MY FATHER, dated April 1943, contained such important news that my mother read parts of it to me as a way of explaining a change that might be about to happen in our lives.

> *In my recent trip to Shen Wei I met a Swiss missionary who has gener-*
> *ously agreed to use his own uncensored neutral country channels to*
> *send this letter to you. Because of this I am able to explain a little more*
> *about the work I am doing and let you know about a sudden change*
> *in my circumstances. I can also enclose a photo—this one taken of me*
> *recently with my Chinese team.*
>
> *Unfortunately, it is a group I will no longer be working with. For*
> *reasons that baffle me, my commanding officer has decided to close the*
> *school I have been developing with the Chinese army to train guerrilla*
> *troops as demolition squads. I am to turn over all our supplies and rec-*
> *ords to an American team and to report to the embassy in Chungking*
> *for my new assignment. As you may have guessed from what little I*
> *could say in my earlier letters I am very proud of the work I have done*
> *here and am terribly disappointed to be leaving it behind. Some kind of*
> *political decision has been made that I don't as yet understand.*
>
> *There is a bright spot in this development. In Chungking I will be*
> *working with Findlay Andrew, our old friend from Cheefoo, who is now*
> *head of intelligence at the Embassy. It will be a lot of meetings and maneu-*
> *verings with the Chinese brass and spy agencies, hardly what I envisioned*
> *when I signed up for the army, BUT it may mean that I can arrange for*
> *you to come and join me there! Wouldn't that be marvelous, darling!*

Of course, I listened to this plan with some anxiety. Where would I be while my mother was in Chungking with my father?

Leaving New York

A T THE END OF MY SPRING TERM at St. George's School in 1944, when I was about to turn ten, my mother got a cable from my father telling her that he had been successful in arranging for her to join him in Chungking. He had made arrangements through the British Embassy in Washington for all transportation, the trains across the continent from Vancouver to New York and a ship from New York to India, and for me to be enrolled in a boarding school in Darjeeling. It was another sudden dislocation, but my mother convinced me that it would be an exciting adventure and a chance to see my father again.

I was a little worried about that future reunion because of all the speculation in my father's letters that I had been transformed into "a strong little fellow" who had made progress in math. I kept my mind focused on the white tigers I hoped to see in India.

In New York we stayed at the Pennsylvania Hotel. Because of heavy security surrounding all ship schedules in order to reduce the risk of submarine attack, my mother was not given a fixed departure day or time. Rather she was told never to be away from the telephone in the hotel room for more than three hours. Once the shipping company called to give us the sailing time we had to be at the dock very quickly. On July 8, after a few days of entertaining ourselves in short bursts away from the hotel, the phone call came telling us when and where to meet the ship.

It was a passenger freighter that had been outfitted with cannons fore and aft, camouflage paint and all the necessary blackout curtains so that it might sail unseen during the night. The passenger part of the ship had been booked to capacity and the four-bunk cabins had been assigned by gender, so my mother and I were in separate quarters. The sense of secrecy, the presence of the cannons and a few military guards gave me a feeling of foreboding. The vessel was awkwardly outfitted to be a ship of war and did not really seem adequate to meet any actual challenge that might lie ahead.

The Bombing Scare

THE PASSENGERS ON THE SHIP were an odd combination of missionaries returning to the Far East, officers rejoining their units, and wives, like my mother, on the way back to husbands; it made for an awkward social life. I spent my days reading in the lounge or occasionally playing shuffleboard with the ship's purser.

The ship took a long, looping, evasive southern route rather than the more direct line to Capetown, our first stop, to avoid the ocean areas in which German submarine activity had been most reported. It meant that the whole trip took thirty-four days rather than twenty. One night in our third week aboard, as the ship approached the horn of Africa, the full up-and-down wail of the emergency siren woke the passengers. We all grabbed our life vests and proceeded to our designated lifeboat stations, just as we had been taught to do in the staged drills. When I moved through the blackout curtain to reach the deck, the blinding white light of a chemical flare illuminated the sky and ship. A plane had dropped the flare, as a first step to bombing the ship. I looked around in a panic to find my mother, but she was nowhere to be seen. It turned out that someone had taken her life jacket and she was still inside the cabin frantically searching for another. She came out on the deck, finally, and a crewmember reached into one of the lifeboats and found her an extra jacket.

My mother and I lined up with our group and waited to step into the lifeboat as the sound of the plane, nearer now and then farther away, circled the blackness above the flare's cone of light. Suddenly a ship's officer ran past, shouting to the crew to stop the evacuation and to crank the lifeboats back up. He announced that the plane had broken radio silence to get a firm identification of the ship before proceeding to bomb and that the plane turned out to be American. Apparently, the pilot thought we were German because our southerly route was so unusual and we were not traveling in convoy, the normal pattern for American ships. Disaster was narrowly averted.

The Garden on Malabar Hill

THERE WAS CONFUSION AT THE DOCKS at Bombay. My father was not there to meet us, nor had his instructions made it through. We gathered our luggage together and stood on the quay wondering what to do. At last my mother remembered that her son Bob had become close to the London family of his best friend in the RAF, Denis Stone, and that Denis's father, Sir Leonard Stone, was now the Chief Judge of the Court in Bombay. My mother had never been shy of using contacts. When she needed a favor she became seductive "Little Rosie," figuratively or actually laying her head on the shoulder of an important man and asking for special dispensation. It worked again. The harbormaster found her the number for Sir Leonard and shortly after her "girl-in-distress" phone call, a large car arrived to take us to a luxurious bungalow on Malabar Hill.

That first afternoon of our stay with the Stones, I got my initial taste of the reality of exotic India. I went out to the beautiful gardens to walk around. The gardener watched me bouncing a ball along one of the paths and ran into the house. Soon the head servant came out and told me very politely that I must play on the verandahs and not among the flowers. It turned out that the gardener had spotted two kraits, extremely poisonous snakes, on the garden paths. Since these small vipers lie in the sun and straighten their bodies out into what look like pretty sticks, I might have been tempted to pick them up or could have sent them into attack mode with my bouncing ball.

On the second day, my mother managed to establish contact with my father through a cable to Chungking. He cabled back that we were to travel by train and then car to Srinagar, in Kashmir, where we would stay on a houseboat with George Findlay Andrew, my father's boss in the Chungking intelligence unit, until he could meet us. What he had explained in the original message that never got through to my mother was that he was in the middle of an important operation in Chungking. We would have to wait another month for the reunion.

The Upper Bunk

OUR COMPARTMENT ON THE TRAIN to Rawalpindi contained two bunk beds, a small table and a chair, a sink, a toilet and a shower. For the first two nights, my mother slept in the top bunk and I in the bottom. On the third night, she decided she wanted to sit up in the chair and read, so she put me in the top bunk. In the middle of the night I forgot where I was, rolled out of the bunk to go to the bathroom, and fell the six feet to the floor, catching the side of my head on the metal corner of the table. It sliced open a gash between my cheek and my ear and produced a good amount of blood. My mother woke to my screams and pulled the emergency cord in the compartment, since there was no central corridor that she could have run into for help, and the train stopped. A large group of Indians gathered next to the tracks outside the compartment door, with nothing to offer but their curiosity. Fortunately, my mother had made friends with the British officer in the next compartment, and he came over with his orderly, who had had first aid training. The soldier cleaned my wound as best he could with Listerine but told my mother that I would need to be stitched up. The conductor said that he could wire ahead to have an ambulance waiting at the next stop, Delhi.

The military ambulance took my mother and me to the Red Fort Hospital, part of the British garrison. The doctor there told my mother that she couldn't stay in the room where the procedure was to take place. He asked an officer to show her to a waiting room. It soon became clear why. They had no anesthetic, or none to waste on a noncombatant, so the stitching on my head was done while three orderlies held me down. I later found out that the officer accompanying my mother kept leading her farther and farther away from the operating room, walking her through as many courtyards as he could.

The Houseboat

AFTER I RECUPERATED IN A DELHI HOTEL FOR THREE DAYS, my mother and I, my head wrapped so that the bandages looked very much like a turban, got back on the train for Rawalpindi. There, we took a long taxi ride through the mountains to the lake city of Srinagar.

For both my mother and me, Srinagar represented all the authentic exoticness of India that we had only imagined back in Vancouver. That Indian authenticity was somewhat undercut when we boarded a water taxi with "Hot to Trot" painted on its bow to take us to Findlay Andrew's houseboat. This was typical of cheeky names, including "Kilroy Was Here" and "Ants in Your Pants," that tourist GIs had encouraged the owners to paint on their craft. When we got to Findlay Andrew's houseboat, however, it was resplendent with true Moghul-style decoration.

We lived for a month on the well-staffed houseboat. The cook and the other servants lived on their own attached houseboat. Small boats arrived frequently, delivering the groceries as well as dealers with curios to sell and, once, a fortune-teller. Findlay was a solicitous host and arranged for us to take a tour of the lake palaces and a carpet-making establishment. I was fascinated by carpets that changed color as they were held up to the light at different angles. The carpets were too expensive for my mother, but she bought small decorative objects, such as sandalwood cigarette boxes and figurines.

There was a small *shikara*, a kind of elegant canoe, that came with the houseboat, which I was allowed to take out on my own. I loved to paddle and glide over the shallow parts of the lake, watching the underwater world, grasses undulating to the passing of my boat and schools of small fish moving in staccato bursts. I felt brave steering my *shikara* far away from the houseboat and my mother.

After a month, we left the houseboat with Findlay and traveled with him by train. He got off at Meerut, where he had meetings at British intelligence headquarters, while my mother and I continued on to Calcutta, where we caught the small-gauge train up the steep mountains to Darjeeling.

Be a Man!

MY FATHER, NOW A LIEUTENANT COLONEL and resplendent in his uniform, met us at the train station in Darjeeling. From there a driver took us to Prativa Lodge. More than three years had gone by in which our experiences had been radically different. I was aware of my father's evaluating gaze, though he did his best to put me at ease.

The next day Mother and Father took me to St. Paul's School to enroll me. We then spent a few days together, going into the town for meals and seeing a movie. I think my mother, too, felt a little like the probationer being watched by her husband for signs of a drinking problem, but she was on her best behavior. Gradually the conversations became easier as we all exchanged memories of Cheefoo. My father's gaunt handsomeness and his serious demeanor made it obvious to my mother and me that he was the one who had endured the real privations and risk in the war while we had led relatively sheltered and privileged lives in Canada. I think it added to the guilt we were both feeling that we had not lived up to his expectations.

At last the day came for students to start the term at St. Paul's. My mother, my father and I congregated on the central quadrangle of the school, along with other parents saying good-bye to their sons. When our good-byes had been spoken and the kisses and hugs administered, I suddenly realized that my mother, the only fixed point in my uncentered life, was about to leave me in India, in totally unfamiliar circumstances, and go with my father to another country. I broke down in sobs and clutched her. Lieutenant Colonel McMullan was acutely embarrassed by my behavior and said, "Oh, for God's sakes, be a man!" There were probably no orders that he had given as an officer that would resonate as powerfully through the years as those few words. After my mother did what she could to comfort me, my parents left.

Calisthenics

M Y MOTHER WAS SOMEWHAT VAGUE about where I was in my educational progress because it had been so broken up, but the headmaster decided to put me in the fourth form. He also decided that I should live in his house, reserved for boys whose parents were in another country or who were, in some other way, a special case. Maybe I was both.

St. Paul's was very strict, and I was caned twice, once for losing my umbrella, and once, with three other boys, for breaking into a locked cupboard to get at the sweets that our parents had sent. But somehow the spirit of the school made life there more than tolerable. The food was atrocious, so-called meat stews that were mostly turnips, and bread that was so gray and sodden that it turned easily into rocklike pellets that were surreptitiously sent zinging around the dining room. All the boys yearned for cakes and cookies, not the amorphous pudding that was served at almost every meal. In the headmaster's house dormitory, one of the "special case" boys was the son of the local maharajah, and each evening a bearer from his father's palace brought him steaming containers of rice, chicken, lamb and decorative desserts. We boys tried to soothe our jealousy by harassing the chubby prince and hiding his slippers, causing him to walk around the dormitory crying out "Where are my sleepers?" which, of course, gave us cruel boys the opportunity to anoint him with the name Sleepers.

In the mornings we did calisthenics out on the big playing field. I was fine with calisthenics, since they didn't involve being upside down and they were done in a physical environment that I found very beautiful. The field had been cut into the hillside so that one edge of it dropped down to the valley below. The view across the field seemed to take you straight to Kanchenjunga and its neighboring Himalayas with only the distant minor hills intervening. Sometimes when the peaks were lit with a particularly glorious gold and pink sunrise, it sent my mind into an esthetic stupor and I found myself called out for not doing my jumping jacks in the same rhythm as the other boys.

The Best Friend

INTENSE FRIENDSHIPS OCCUPIED much of the psychological energy of the school. I was deeply involved in maintaining a "best friendship" with a handsome, athletic boy named Neil Worman. This consisted of walking together around the school with our arms around each other's shoulders, confessing secrets and acknowledging our special connection. I attended to the relationship a little more avidly than Worman, who had the insouciance of being on the soccer team, but I used my growing skill at copying characters out of comic books to keep Worman intrigued.

Alas, my artistic seductions turned out to be not enough. After a month, Worman announced that his previous best friend had returned to the school after recovering from a broken arm (suffered, no doubt, as a soccer teammate) and that he must transfer the "best friend" designation back to his former buddy. In this all-or-nothing world I was left to get along in the shifting alliances among the boys who didn't inspire emotional ownership.

Comic books, too, were objects of intense interest at St. Paul's. They were very expensive, hard to find and passed around (very carefully) among a select group of aficionados. I was one of three boys who drew well enough to be given extra time to study the pages and produce copies that could be judged. The other two artists were obsessed with drawing Superman, but I was more interested in offbeat characters like The Phantom and Green Lantern. The slight crudeness in the delineation of The Phantom particularly intrigued me because it seemed more suggestive and mysterious than the explicitness of Superman. The audience for these drawings didn't quite understand my fascination with minor heroes, but fortunately I could also produce a plausible Wonder Woman, so I was able to maintain my standing.

What I missed in India was seeing the *Saturday Evening Post*. In Salt Spring, I spent hours scrutinizing the magazine, studying the details in the covers by Norman Rockwell and of all the illustrations inside. The magazine gave me my earliest conception of the career of an illustrator and, better yet, an illustrator who told emotional stories.

Getting the News

MY PARENTS WERE TOO FAR AWAY to visit me during the various holidays, so I didn't see them for almost a year after the difficult moment when we had said good-bye.

On August 15, 1945, Japan surrendered. We boys were called out to the quadrangle for the announcement and encouraged to give a loud "Hip, Hip, Hooray!" For dessert at dinner we were served coconut cake as a special treat.

About a month after that I was called out of class to meet a serious-looking young officer who introduced himself as a friend of my father's and said he would like to treat me to an ice cream Sundae at the café in Darjeeling. We walked down the hill into the town, the officer trying his best to make small talk. At the restaurant, after I had eaten most of my ice cream, the officer said that he had some bad news; my father had been killed in a plane crash. He told me that my father had been flying back from overseeing the repatriation of British internees from a Japanese prisoner-of-war camp and the plane had crashed into a mountain during a storm. He put his arms around me and told me that I could cry, but I had retreated into numbness and I could not think or cry.

The hill back to school seemed steeper than it ever had before, and I had to concentrate on putting one foot in front of the other. At the school, my English composition teacher, my favorite, put me in his lap and stroked my head, repeating "Cry, Jimmie, cry." But I could not cry and I could not make sense of my conflicted feelings. I knew, then, that my deep longing for a father would never be satisfied, but on the other hand, I realized that I would not again have to face my father's disappointment in me and that I would have my mother to myself. I was overwhelmed with shame that I could not feel a pure love for my father, nor sadness for his death.

The teacher helped me pack up my few belongings, and the young officer and I took the train to Calcutta.

General Sir Adrian Carton de Wiart

THROUGH HIS WORK IN INTELLIGENCE and as the military attaché in Chung-king, my father had made many friends in high places. On the news of his death and hearing of my need to join my mother, one of these friends, General Sir Adrian Carton de Wiart, King George's envoy in Asia, arranged for me to stay at the Governor of Bengal's residence in Calcutta prior to being flown in the general's plane to Chungking.

When I arrived at the residence, I was shown to the Lawrence of Arabia suite and then offered a tour of the garage. Gleaming black ceremonial Daimlers with their stanchions for the governor's flag and the Union Jack were arranged in a row. The chauffeur started one of the cars and invited me to sit behind the steering wheel and work the button that made the glass partition between the front and back seats go up and down. Sitting in that huge car that day was as much distraction as an eleven-year-old boy in a state of shock could ask for.

In the evening I was taken to the main salon to meet the governor, his wife and General Carton de Wiart. The general was a sight to be seen, tall and commanding, one sleeve of his uniform pinned up neatly where his left arm had once been, his missing left eye covered in a black patch and his strong nose standing guard over a vigorous mustache. The parade of ribbons on his chest attested to his being the most decorated general in the British army. He told me how much he admired my father and, against all the evidence of the hesitant boy standing in front of him, said he was confident that I would grow up to be just like my heroic dad. The adults went in to dinner and I returned to my room to be served a solitary meal of roast beef and carrots, followed by chocolate ice cream.

The Flight

BEFORE DAWN THE NEXT MORNING, the general and I were driven to Dum Dum Airport, just outside the city. Warming up on the tarmac was the general's DC-3, an American-produced plane that was well suited for the long flights required of this roving British military ambassador. It was also the best aircraft for "flying the Hump," the six-hour trip over the Himalayas and into China that we were about to make on this, my first time on an airplane. Other than the three-man crew, the general and I were the only people aboard. I was assigned a seat far back from the general's. He gave me a quasimilitary assignment appropriate for a boy, telling me to report the time to him every two hours. The interior of the plane was noisy and cold, but I bundled up in a blanket and concentrated on my time-alerting duties—and also obsessively watched the mountains below us to see that we didn't come too close.

After I had walked up the aisle three times to make my two-hourly report and was rewarded by the general's curt "Very good!" the drone of the plane's engines ground a little softer and we started our descent into Kunming, the refueling stop before the final leg of the journey to Chungking.

At the airport in Kunming we were met by my cousin Lieutenant Bob Mc-Mullan, who, coincidentally, had just been assigned to begin his job as the general's aide-de-camp. Bob conveyed his reserved English sympathy to me, "Sorry, old chap, about your dad," the plane was refueled, and the three of us flew on to Chungking, where my mother was waiting.

The Crazy City

MY MOTHER HAD TAKEN THE SUDDEN DEATH of my father very hard. For this tragic accident to have happened just as the war had ended, after my father had survived those years behind the lines when my mother had not known for months on end whether he was alive or dead, seemed like an unimaginably cruel twist of fate. For the first few days after I arrived, my mother was an emotional mess. She constantly hugged and kissed me, and her physical neediness undercut any sense that she was in control. Fortunately, Findlay Andrew came forward to help her get through the panic she must have been feeling. He was preparing to leave his official post as head of British Intelligence in Chungking and move to Shanghai, where he had arranged to become an adviser to several companies, including Butterfield & Swire, the British shipping company. The company had provided him with a house in its compound in the French concession, and he convinced Rose that she and I should go to Shanghai to live with him for a while.

We flew with Findlay to Shanghai and set ourselves up in his house on Avenue Haig. I was enrolled in the British/American School, which was within biking distance of the house. Set out along my route to the school were coffins waiting for the almost nonexistent city services to eventually pick them up. These manifestations of the breakdown of civil services gave me the feeling that the city was in a state of barely controlled chaos. We heard stories of how the police knocked on people's doors, and when they opened them, gangs of thieves hiding behind the police burst in to rob the house. The relatively small force of U.S. Military Police established whatever ragged sense of order there was in the city. It was a mood of "anything goes." An American pilot whom Findlay knew was using his air force plane to fly currency around the country to take advantage of different rates of exchange. Across the street from his house, what was, before the war, the most elite nightclub in Shanghai had been turned into a barely disguised house of prostitution.

My Mother's Admirers

MY MOTHER, A DEPRESSIVE ON THE DEEPEST LEVEL of her personality, was nonetheless always ready for a drink and a party. In the freewheeling atmosphere of Shanghai just after the war, there was much frenetic socializing, and these opportunities for distraction helped her get over, or at least momentarily forget, her grief at my father's death. Also, because Findlay Andrew was a man connected to all the politicians and military brass of any consequence in the city's society, the house we shared with him was a crossroads for interesting encounters. Europeans such as General Carton de Wiart and the British ambassador had a chance to share canapés with ministers from the newly formed Chinese Nationalist cabinet. Findlay also had many old friends from his years as an explorer who came by the house. I never understood whether these explorations that Findlay had made in the past were scientific or political ventures, but they seemed to have set him up as a master spy in Chungking.

Before long, Rose McMullan, the attractive and vivacious widow who played hostess for Findlay's soirées, was being noticed by many of the men who were a long way from home and from their wives. Two naval officers, in particular, took turns coming to the house to pay court.

On many evenings, a long, black, chauffer-driven Packard, its trunk customized to hold two crouching armed guards, brought an American admiral to the house to have drinks with my mother or to take her to his flagship for dinner. The car, custom-made in 1939 for a Chinese warlord, had been confiscated by the Japanese and was now a perk for the admiral. I remember him as a brash, extremely confident man who made it clear that he was Texan through and through. A slightly more subdued officer, a commodore, arrived on other evenings in a simple Buick staff car to take my mother dancing or to a fancy Chinese restaurant where she could play expert about the cuisine.

On these evenings I was presented at cocktail hour just long enough for these macho Americans to take my measure.

Across the River

AT ONE OF THE SCHOOL HOLIDAYS, my mother arranged for me to stay aboard a river steamer, the *Marguerite*, on the far side of the Yangtze. The *Marguerite* was between shipping jobs and none of the crew, except for the captain, seemed to be around. It was the second time in my life, after my explorations alone in the *shikara* in Srinagar, that I actually had unstructured time ahead of me and was assumed by an adult not to need supervision. At first the freedom was daunting and I only wandered around the decks near my cabin. When the sky didn't fall, I checked out all the other decks and finally walked down the gangplank and onto the dock.

Farther down the dock I saw another interesting ship, so I decided to take a closer look. When I got to it a young man in a khaki uniform asked if I was the boy he'd heard was staying on the *Marguerite*. When I said yes, he introduced himself as Jonathan, the engineer of the ship, and asked if I would like to see the engine room. I followed Jonathan up the gangplank, through the many corridors and down into the engine room. As I navigated the steep ladder that once might have given me vertigo, I was too excited to be scared and would have been embarrassed to show any kind of fear in front of Jonathan. After looking at all the boilers and gauges and pistons and signal boxes, it was time for me to go back to the *Marguerite* for dinner. Jonathan said that I could come back the next morning if I wanted and he would show me more of the ship.

I was at Jonathan's cabin early the next day. He showed me the wheelhouse, the captain's deck, the dining room and the engines for lifting containers into the hold. For two more days, I tagged along behind Jonathan while he did his engineer chores. He was bemused by my obvious hero-worship and not completely surprised by a four-stanza poem called "Friendship" that I had been inspired to write and which I solemnly presented to him on my last afternoon of staying on that side of the river.

Mr. Ryan

ONE RESULT OF MY MOTHER'S DATES with the admiral and the commodore was that she got a lot of advice on how to raise me. Both men were convinced that she was too indulgent and soft on me and that, as a result, I had become a timid boy heading straight into the dark valley of effeminacy. They both advised the same cure: boxing lessons. My mother seemed to have forgotten that this prescription for building manliness had already failed with my boxing lessons in Grand Forks.

The lessons were on Saturday, taught by an ex-flyweight contender from Australia, Mr. Ryan. He was in his late forties but still in stringy-muscled trim. He started the class of seven boys by having us jog in place and then he demonstrated the various kinds of punches. We boys put on our gloves and then were matched up by height to try some actual sparring.

I think I tried hard to land some punches and I was able to move around fairly fast, but after the third matchup it had become clear that I was not able to deflect or duck the enthusiastic blows that were landed on my head and ribs. My head rang, my sides ached and I felt humiliated. I sat down on the bench and concentrated on not allowing the tears that were welling up inside me to fall. That would be my triumph for the day. At the end of the class, Ryan approached and said, "Let's go for a walk, Jimmie."

In the schoolyard, as we walked side by side, Ryan asked, in a surprisingly gentle voice, "Not too keen on sports, eh, Jimmie?"

"No," I replied, my voice constricted.

Ryan put his hand on my shoulder, "Well, I'll tell your mum it's not the right class for you. By the way, what do you like to do?"

"I like to draw, Mr. Ryan."

"Well then," he said, smiling down at me, "you'll be an artist and not a boxer."

This act of kindness opened the floodgates, and I cried quietly as we walked to the door. Mr. Ryan left his hand on my shoulder until we said good-bye.

On *the* USS Breckenridge

M Y MOTHER HAD REALIZED FROM THE START that there was no real future for us in Shanghai. The Nationalist army was losing the fight against the Communists under Mao Ze-dong, and it would be only a matter of time before the city was taken over by Mao's forces. There was a great crush of people trying to get to America and England, but we managed to find passage on a ship leaving for San Francisco. The USS *Breckenridge* was a troop carrier that had a reserved section for civilians. The accommodations were spartan, dormitory-style cabins with the bunks three high and not much room between them, but my mother accepted that this was the only option on the horizon and that her days of luxury liners were over.

She packed up our belongings, Findlay threw a good-bye party, and my mother and I found ourselves on a crowded dock once more, making our way up a gangplank and onto a ship. We were directed to separate male and female cabins.

We met in the morning for breakfast in the navy-style cafeteria and then walked out to the deck for some fresh air. As we leaned on the railing, looking out to sea, I was overcome with the feeling that my mother and I were two survivors who, in the eleven years of my life, had been through hard times together. It was the closest I had felt to her in a long time, but also, strangely, the most separate. All the experiences of moving from one place to another and somehow enduring the dislocation and all the strangeness and bullying, mostly alone, had made me sense the beginning of a life where I would increasingly look after myself (and even her) and I would also discover values of my own.

My mother turned to me and asked, "What are you looking forward to, Jimmie?"

I thought for a moment. "I would like to go back to Salt Spring."

She replied, "I've already written to Ella, asking if we can come back to stay with them. I can't imagine she'll say no."

We walked a little more and I was smiling as the ship churned through the waves, sailing steadily east.

All the Rest, Very Briefly

MY MOTHER AND I DID GO BACK to live with the Wilsons on Salt Spring Island. Very soon, she met and married her third husband. He turned out to be a violent man and she divorced him. But even though the idyll that Salt Spring represented was short lived, the Wilsons' house on the water continued to exist in my mind as a kind of beautiful sanctuary. Many years later I was able to buy a modest house on a tranquil cove in Sag Harbor, Long Island, that, to this day, re-creates the emotional centeredness I felt living with the Wilsons.

We emigrated to the United States when I graduated high school in Canada, and after serving in the American army, I moved to New York to study art at Pratt Institute. In my early years as an illustrator, my most significant work was probably book jackets, because they reflected how much I was attracted to literary material, a turn of mind I later used to create theater posters. Achieving vitality in drawing has always been a central objective of my work, inspired by the vigor of the drawing in the Chinese scrolls I studied in Cheefoo, and it led me to teach life classes at the School of Visual Arts for many years.

Along the way I married Kate Hall, a vivacious children's-book writer, and a little later, our daughter, Leigh, was born. Reading to Leigh when she was young motivated me to illustrate the stories Kate was writing and started us on a collaboration that has produced twelve books so far, including the kid favorite, *I Stink!*, a monologue by a garbage truck.

I continue to design posters for Lincoln Center Theater and to create picture books with Kate. After forty years of dividing our time between Manhattan and the country, we now live in Sag Harbor full time. I have even become moderately athletic as a tennis player. It's not exactly wiping out my gymnastic or boxing histories, but after I triumph in one of my doubles matches, I imagine Mr. Ryan standing on the sidelines, giving me a thumbs-up.

Acknowledgments

I have had much for which to be grateful during the years that it has taken for this book to come into being. The people who have made it possible are like an informal team in which each member, at various stages, contributed something in a way no one else could have done. Looking back, I marvel at how indispensable each person was in helping to launch a book that did not fit neatly into any known category and depended so much on the acceptance of the writing and the pictures for their own curious nature.

Writing the story and painting the images for this book was an endeavor so far out of the regular stream of my life that the early encouragement I received was particularly crucial. My first drafts of the text might have led someone else to advise abandonment, but my wife, Kate, read these efforts and saw me through my struggles to find a voice for the narrator and give me, at that fragile moment, essential feedback and hope. Holly McGhee, my friend and literary agent, also read early drafts and made amazingly intuitive and clarifying suggestions of how I might better shape the history I was writing.

Holly's experience in the publishing world and her sensitivity to the nature of my project led her to make a remarkable connection—to introduce me to Elise Howard at Algonquin Young Readers. Within minutes of my meeting Elise I knew that I was unbelievably lucky to have this extraordinary and responsive person editing and publishing my book. My first impression has been more than fulfilled. Not only have Elise's inspired ideas for the book and her editing clarified its unique characteristics, but also she chose a particularly auspicious guide to help me make all those small (and not so small) text improvements and reconsiderations of the art.

That guide has been the remarkable editor and painter Joanna Cotler. My previous experience with Joanna, as editor of three of Kate's and my picture books, established between us a great friendship and mutual respect, so that working with Joanna on this book was as sympathetic and productive a process

112

as I could possibly imagine. Joanna's participation has felt to me like going on a journey with a fellow artist, rather than simply finding better words for the sentences.

Elise has given me even more creative support by having the brilliant idea of engaging a designer from three of my previous books, Neil Swaab. Not only does Neil have extraordinary taste and graphic imagination, he has exhibited great sensitivity to the nature of my art. His design choices for *Leaving China* have again exhibited his harmonious connection to the color and rhythms of my paintings.

Judit Bodnar brought an astounding level of attention and intelligence to the process of copyediting *Leaving China*. She found many slips of grammar that the rest of us had missed, but she also questioned basic meanings within sentences and paragraphs. Without her several queries in the margin—"Do you mean . . . ?"—and the rethinking that ensued, the book would have been a little less coherent. I am also indebted to Julie Primavera, who oversaw the complexities of putting this very visual book together and, with her eagle eye for color, was indispensable in making corrections to the several rounds of color proofs. I want to thank Emily Parliman, who, with her good spirit and many clear e-mails to all of us, kept the train on the track through more than a year of interweaving tasks and instructions.

Writing this story and painting these pictures has been one of the most significant and rewarding experiences of my life. Along with all the advice, editing, and creative choices you all generously contributed to the publication of *Leaving China*, you also recognized the book's special place in my life, and for that I am deeply grateful.

Cheefoo

Salt Spring Island   Vancouver

Seattle   Grand
          Forks

Shanghai

San Francisco